Pencils on Strike
Copyright © 2021 Jennifer Jones
All copyright laws and rights reserved.
Published in the U.S.A.
For more information, email jenniferjonesbooks@gmail.com
ISBN: 978-1-63731-274-2

The most unappreciated things
Are usually the most used.
These utensils are usually
Lost and abused.

This is the story of a group of pencils
That are so often overlooked,
The kind of important tool needed
To write in a notebook!

Few people think about
How hard a pencil's life is.
We help all students,
Especially the math whiz.

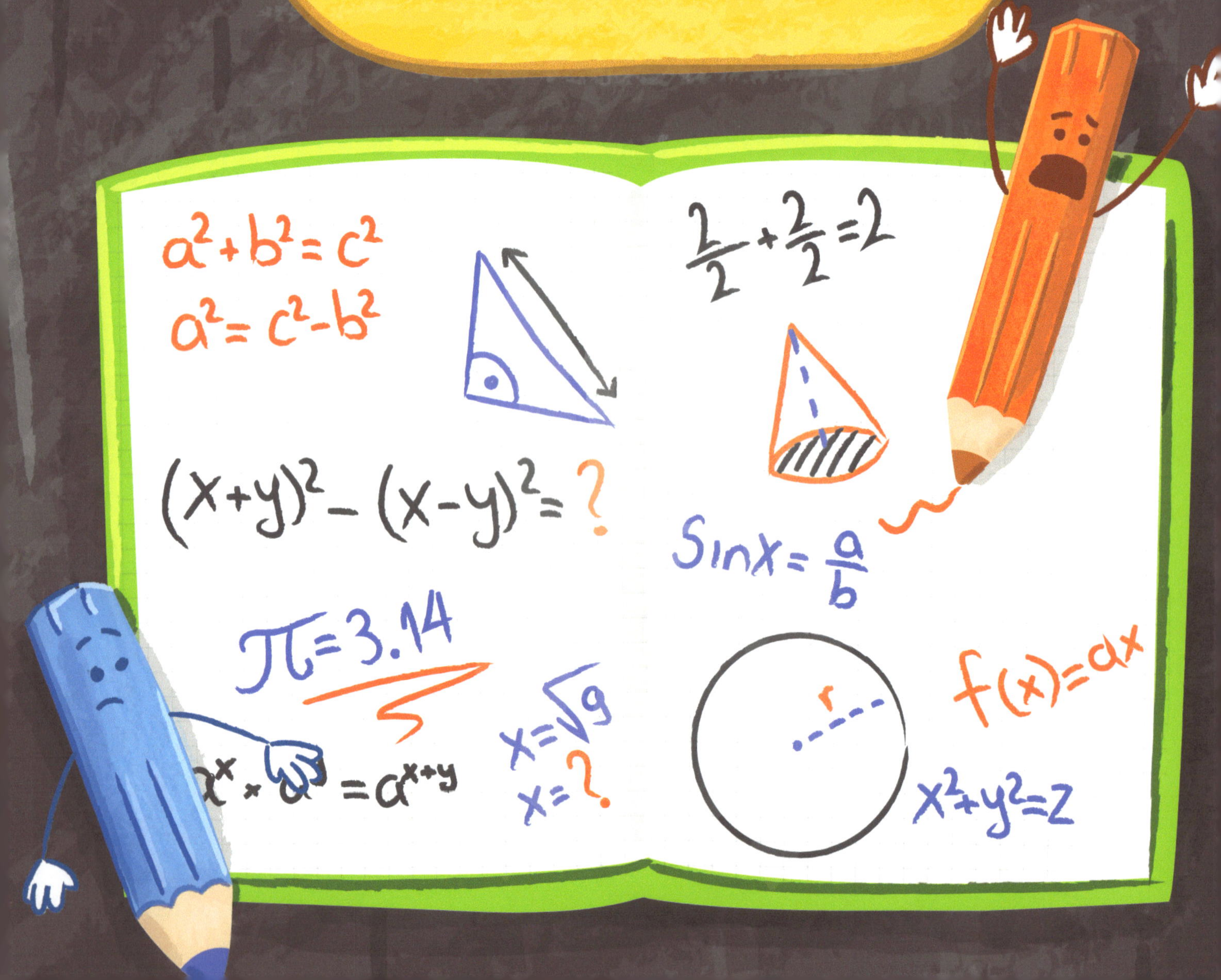

Our ability is to capture thoughts
And translate them onto paper.
But no! Our importance has not
At all kept us safer.

So when the students were at lunch,
And we were laid to rest.
We got together
And we did what we do best.

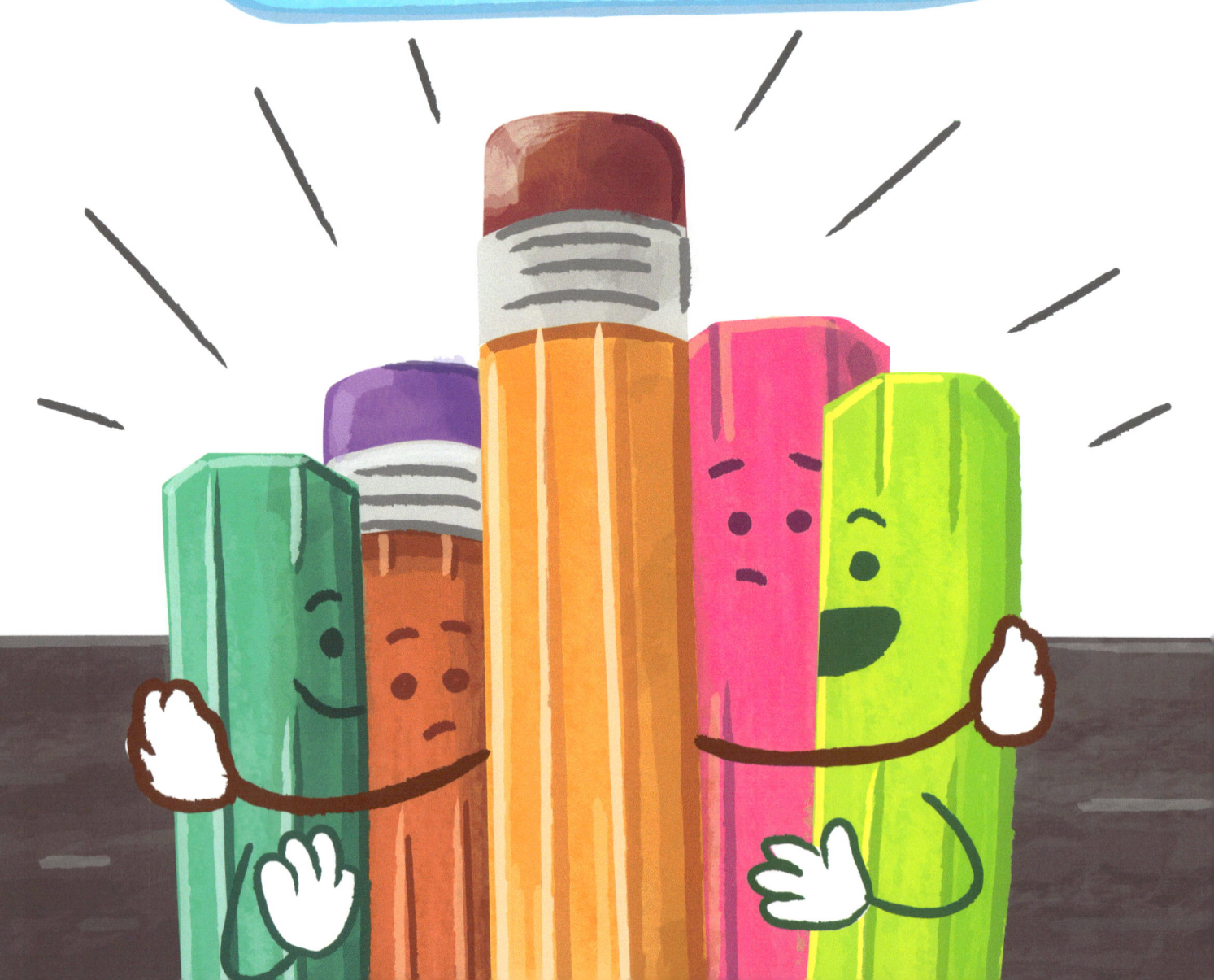

We aired our complaints
And wrote a letter just to be clear.
We had some grievances
For the students to hear.

Students, we're here to tell you
That we're sick of being tossed around,
Rolled around, snapped in half,
Or left to fall hard on the ground.

We're chewed on and held in mouths
As if we had just fought.
Our erasers are bent or bit off,
Often without a second thought.

And not to mention the snapping
That you sometimes do with us for fun.
You carelessly toss us aside
When you feel our work is finally done.

But how often is it that you see
A pencil get used gently at school?
So much of us gets wasted
Despite us being such an important tool.

"They're right," she said.
"We should treat our pencils better.
Come on now, grab a pencil,
Let's practice it together."

And one by one, the students
Handled us with more care.
All it took was a letter to make
Everything good and fair.

CPSIA information can be obtained
at www.ICGtesting.com
Printed in the USA
BVHW021053110822
644348BV00008B/219